The Perfect Night

The Perfect Night

Tej Ashish

Copyright © 2009 Tej Ashish

ISBN 978-0-9563459-0-5

Contents

Bewilderment	1
The Perfect Night	3
Pain	5
Oh, Leiden!	11
Life	13
Touch!	15
Stormy Night	17
Why Be Happy?	21
No Hope	23
You Don't Love Me For …	29
The Light at the End of the Tunnel	31
Is There Another World We Can Go To?	33
Eternal Love	35
Have We Arrived?	37

Flying in bewilderment? They're all hovering to grab the not so distinct pieces of bread floating on the water

1

Bewilderment

Bewilderment, anger, hatred, and pain
Come to me when I think of anything but your name.
It's amazing how I suffer when I think about the mundane,
But your name is not in vain.
Immediately, it gives me strength, confidence, glory,
And a destination where I want to remain.

A full moon lighting a path on a calm sea, a cloudless sky and a gentle breeze: Nature's very own Perfect Night.

2

The Perfect Night

When night falls,
All falls,
Like the sun and the telephone calls.
If the mood is light
And your bed is just right,
Cosy, comfy, and tight,
And you can retire without a fright,
Oh yes, it is the perfect night.

Everything's right,
Not too dull and not too bright.
There, by your bedside,
A cup of warm milk
With coco inside,
A few pages of your favourite book
Before you hit the light,
Oh yes, this is the perfect night.

Slumber comes gently.
As fairies kiss goodnight,
You dream of nothing less
Than satisfying delights.
You wake up refreshed,
With a smile that's bright,
And you cannot help but think,
Oh yes, that was the perfect night.

Another photograph of the same day and reminiscent of the same feelings.

3
Pain

Dear God, thank You for this pain.
It has become a part of my name.
I don't know how to live.
Without this pain I'd crib,
For the moment it goes I'll feel
That life is over and I've lived
A life that's over too quick,
Without the satisfaction that it gives,
And this pain is the antidote to it.

Dear God, thank You for this pain.
My life feels not in vain.
I've learnt all from this pain.
Happiness teaches you to be
A fool that has no pain,
But I don't want to lie to You,
I wish I was a fool
All the time,
Happy and without pain.

Dear God, thank You for this pain,
But all your pain is not the same.
There are pains that are more severe,
that have pained me all my life,
And for no rhyme or reason,
I feel them in every season.

The body language of this cyclist is reminiscent of pain, sorrow and difficulty. I felt it suited the poem quite well.

Tej Ashish

There are wounds that they leave.
They make me want some place just to be able to breathe,
And they make me put up my hands and say please, help.

Dear God, thank You for this pain,
But you must explain to me time and again
Why you turn on the tap and forget,
For there's someone who's getting soaking wet.
All the tears that come down my cheeks,
All the prayers that go past my teeth
Are meant to tell You, look,
There's someone who has to bleed.
Look down and pay some heed.

Dear God, thank You for this pain.
You may not remember what it can do.
You may not remember how it feels,
Because You came long ago,
But I still sit here,
And the pain of life
Keeps me huddled in unease.
No matter how many solutions I find,
You have enough creativity up Your sleeve.

Dear God, thank You for this pain.
It shows me that I cannot remain.
All the achievements that I add to my name
Are with me for just one time frame.
For when I come back into the game,
I must start all over again,

But I am lucky if I get a chance to play.
There are many that don't get to come this way,
And for them, this pain is much too great to say.

Dear God, thank You for this pain,
But please tell me how to stay sane.
The suffering I see is spread over a large plain.
The only tried-and-tested cure, used by generations galore,
Is time and nothing more,
But my suffering is much more than my crime.
So You have a lot of explaining to do.
When You assigned me my quota,
Tell me what You had in mind.

Dear God, thank You for this pain.
However long you want me to wait for an answer,
I know it will not be in vain.
You have grand plans for me after all.
I hope I can wait all the same.
You know impatience has its day, every day,
And faith is not hard to contain,
But I know in the end I will be able to say,
Dear God, thank You indeed for this pain.

A lazy summer afternoon for some, in beautiful Leiden.

4

Oh, Leiden!

Oh, Leiden!
To be as quaint as you,
as quiet as you,
as kind as you,
as beautiful as you,
as petite as you,
as perfect as you

To be as Leiden as you
Is wonderful!

To be with you
Is a dream come true,
But perhaps it is too good to be true,
So admire you from afar is what I shall do,
Oh, Leiden!

5
Life

Why have you given me this life?
Why not a little bit different one?
Okay, why not a little bit easier
Or a bit, shall we say, more in my control,
A little bit lighter?
I've heard so much from other people
Life is what you make of it.
You know I've tried,
Tried always to do what is right.
Still, it's the same; it doesn't look any brighter
Or in my favour.
What a life!

Those whom you have made more fortunate think
They have it in their control.
What do they know; it's something between us.
You just want them to feel like that.
But why? Why not me? Why am I not one of them?
Is it because they are weaker than me and cannot handle the truth?
Let me tell you, I haven't felt stronger than them
Even though you have chosen me to go through so much extra.
Are you hearing me, or am I just talking to myself
About things that don't really matter?

"An orgy of your touch!": I think the tiger on the right expressed it the best.

6

Touch!

The last time I felt a jolt of electricity through me
Was when I felt your touch!
A million watts went through me!
Something about you just blew me!
Normalcy just flew me,
And I craved for one more touch!

The passion grew inside me.
This wonderful thing just knew me.
How could I be so crushed?
It's just the matter of one touch!

Come on now, and just do me.
Don't waste time on the gloomy.
I just want to make you my roomie
And have an orgy of your touch!

This is all so just groovy.
My mind's now spinning around me.
Who knew I had so much lust,
All for just one touch!

This is something that's too much!
So don't get caught in the rush.
No one can value it so much—
The worth of your wholesome touch!

A stormy night grounded this ship off the Aguada beach in Goa. In the foreground is Fort Aguada.

7

Stormy Night

Yes, that is what it was—a stormy night
With lightning so bright and sounds so harsh.
I looked outside as they kept me uptight.
The waves of my sea were all white with fright,
Coming rushing, dashing to the rocks,
Hoping they would help them hide
From the anger of the moon.
Oh, he was out all right!

He came from behind the clouds that he had ridden all night
To bring the storm that stood outside.
He showed his face and then went out of sight.
He was on a mission and not to be a moon gazer's delight.

With his lightning whip he controlled the clouds.
Striking again and again, he made it clear,
Tonight is not a good night, so beware!

It started to pour, and pour it did.
All was wet in a matter of bits.
The clouds ran fast across the sky,
And a hard wind followed close by.

Everything shook, and the windows vibrated.
Come take a look before it's all annihilated,
Shouted the moon with a frown on his brow.

Another photograph of the same ship. I just couldn't get enough of it. It was quite a sight.

Tej Ashish

His confidence was up, and he was on the prowl.

He had a fit as he clamoured for gore.
The thunder roared louder than before.
He ordered the clouds to give it all they had,
To empty the ocean they had brought on their backs.

Hearing this, they left all shame,
Filled the sea till it was no longer mundane.
The sea was now a slave,
Hypnotised by the rain.
It flooded the town in the face of complaints.

The moon was happy and looked with disdain.
It all seemed too easy,
And suddenly, he found it in vain,
Decided to quit because it was fun no more.
He ignored the aftermath as if it was all as before.
This is the story of the night
That left a deep impression out of sheer fright.

This swan looks positively unhappy. Perhaps it doesn't like its picture being taken.

8

Why Be Happy?

Why be happy when there's so much to be sad about?
Happiness doesn't last, sadness does.
When you're in the fleabag of life,
You feel the itch, even if you're rich.

Don't get used to happiness;
It doesn't last.
Get used to sadness;
It'll make you last.

Sadness is great;
It's sadly underrated.
Believe in it and you'll soon be elated.
That's the secret for those who want to make it.

It's not pessimistic;
Ask any great mystic.
Accepting sadness is the key
To a life that is optimistic.

There is no hope when the door leading to the sanctuary of a church or a temple is shut.

9

No Hope

I feel the weight of the skies on my chest.
I see the darkness of dusk before my eyes.
My breath doesn't want to be in me.
The serpent of death scares me
To do nothing and give up.
There is no hope he tells me.
So why don't I follow him and make it easy?
Because my heart tells me what he says is crazy.

No hope to pick up the boulder in my way,
No hope to find another way,
No hope to wake up and say,
It was just a dream; come let's start the day.

I see nothing but gloom in front of me.
This mood will be the death of me.
It seems the serpent has succeeded,
But wait, something in me still wants to try
To find a way. Oh yes, I can fly.
These are the hopes that make me last
The assault of the serpent who wants me to die.

No hope to enjoy the new day,
No hope to retire and pray,
Thank you, God, this was a good day,
Full of work but free from decay.

A sun about to set
offers no hope either

Tej Ashish

There are no opportunities; it's all over.
The good stuff is gone and you are leftover.
Catching up now will not do,
For you are too late. Let go;
It's better for you,
But I've put my shoes on and I want to try.
Let me miss, but let me run.
This is not over till I've begun.

No hope to see me smile,
No hope to feel free again,
You're caught, he says.
This is the end of days, nothing to gain but a lot to pay.

Your deeds are such,
What to say? It's hopeless, so why don't you just stay?
You have left behind all your sway.
The future is too mighty and brave,
Nothing like you will ever be able to face.
Look at me just listening to you rave.
The future is mine, and I don't yet need a grave.
You may think that you have me down on my face,
But I will fight because I'm not your slave.

No hope that's all he ever says,
So much poison and so much haze,
No hope is what he wants to see on my face.
You're worthless, he concludes in a rage.

I cannot express my anger to him,

Without the leaves it all looks like an intricate mesh, dark and bleak.

Tej Ashish

Not because he has venom and wants me to have shame,
But because I feel some weakness in him.
His anger proves that he is insecure.
I can win, and for that he has no cure.
Don't listen to him,
Is what I hear.
Live your dream, only then come to me,
Says the God who protects me.

No hope is never true,
No hope is just fear.
You are my child, and you are free to do
All that you want without fear.

The home of God: A sublimely peaceful church in Leiden.

10

You Don't Love Me For …

You don't love me for my money,
Because you know I don't have any.
You don't love me for my fame,
Because you know it is you who gave me this claim.
You don't love me for my looks,
Because you know they're just not part of the game.
You don't love me for my deeds,
Because you know they are few and far between.
You don't love me for my flesh and blood,
Because that would be a lie and a thud.
You don't even love me because I love you,
Because I didn't know you until recently.
You love me in a way only God can,
Maybe because that's who you are.

A different kind of tunnel at Hampton Court Palace, UK.

11

The Light at the End of the Tunnel

I have lived my life under a cloud of miseries.
Another struggle starts
Before the first one has ended.
The light at the end of the tunnel
Is where the Holy Grail rests.

Even though I have walked and hope to walk some more,
The light at the end of the tunnel
Seems just as elusive as before.

I think this photograph of the back waters of Kerela, India is most apt for conveying what I had in mind regarding this poem.

12

Is There Another World We Can Go To?

Is there another world we can go to,
A world full of bright colours and a beautiful existence,
Where the rain does not dampen the spirits,
Where the sun does not burn the soul,
Where the rainbow has every minute,
And the beautiful water reflects everything in it?

I close my eyes and smile as we step in it,
For there is nothing here to spoil the show.
As we enter the water, we can grip it,
This feeling that is pure as gold.

The vibe is so magnific.
It makes you erase all the bad and the horrific.
Ever wondered what is bliss incarnate?
Here is where you won't miss it.

Every hue caresses the senses,
And every plant has wild and passionate fragrances.
I pray this isn't a dream or a diptych,
For I want to call it home.

Watching a "circus"? Actually watching a Shakespeare play. The photo is a bit blurred, which is a good thing as it makes the scene look like an impressionist painting.

13

Eternal Love

Came to this world I had with a purpose,
Forgot what it was until I found you at this circus
Of life, where everything was bright and happy, but only on the surface.
Now the real meaning of life has sunk in, and it's not as stupid as it first was.
To be with you all the time and experience life as truly sublime is surely a gift and not a tempest.
Come let us realise and specialise the qualities of this outburst
Of love—no, eternal love, for it has to be that to be this tumultuous.
Everything is alive and tearing at its sides. It's unbelievable, and it's tremendous.
With all these emotions inside, it's still all peace and quiet. It's miraculous and not preposterous,
To those who think it's a lie, they are never satisfied and waste time in good-byes.
Chasing after an illusion is the only solution they deem fit, and therefore, they repeat
Their miserable condition of life, which is filled with false obligation.
They have no mercy inside but crave love that is divine. It's a miscalculation,
For love that is divine focuses not on "This is yours, and that is mine." It's beyond objectification.
This is the time. It comes in line and asks you to be mine, and it serves no other purpose.
Everything falls behind, from the dime to the gold mine, and the world becomes this circus,
Which runs after things that exist only to bring on a binge, which results in a cringe,
And they miss out on this surplus of love that abounds in their very background,
Calling them to turn around and showing a new direction on which to be bound.
It's beautiful, that destination, and it's called the eternal love station.

These wild flowers certainly are a beauty.

14

Have We Arrived?

We have come so far together,
Have we arrived?
Hardly.
Rather, this is the beginning
Of a beautiful time spent thinking of you.

We have left behind the problems, miseries, and difficulties.
Have they ended?
Hardly,
But they are less captivating now.
More attractive are the beauties, lilies, and sundries.

www.ingramcontent.com/pod-product-compliance
Ingram Content Group UK Ltd.
Pitfield, Milton Keynes, MK11 3LW, UK
UKHW061139180426
11947UKWH00002B/7